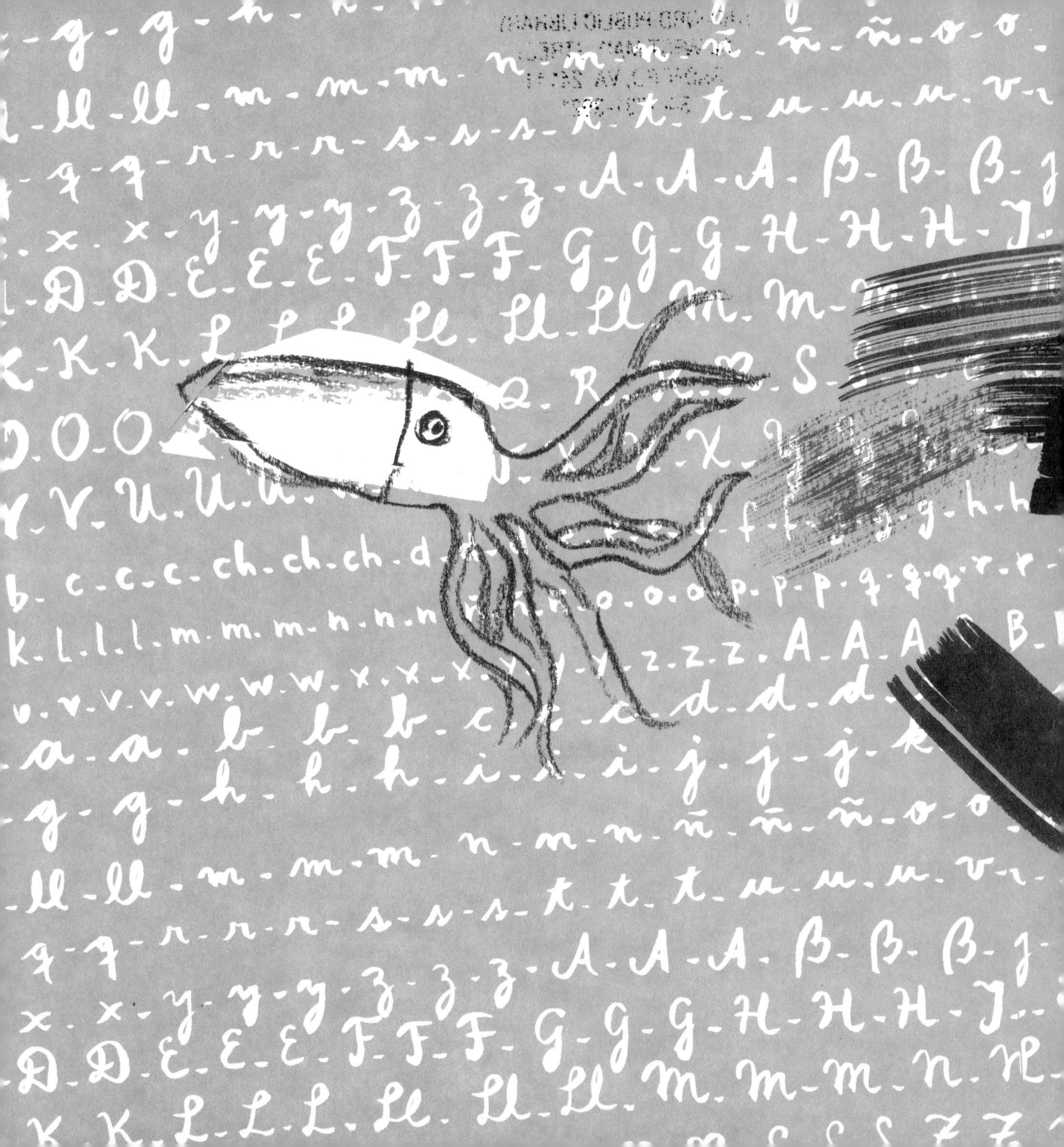

Daytime Visions

An Alphabet

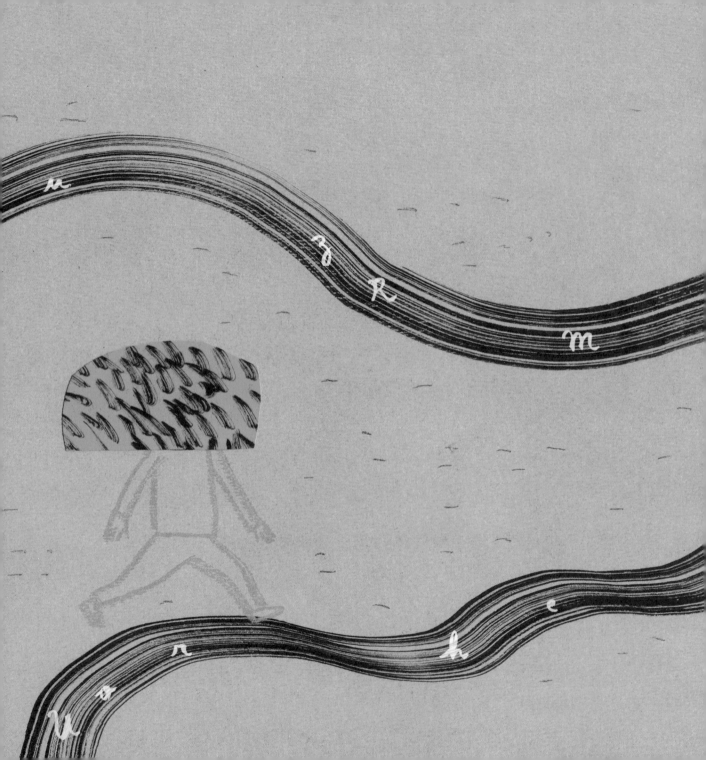

ISOL

DayTime Visions

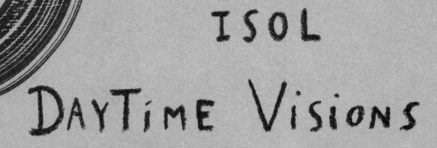

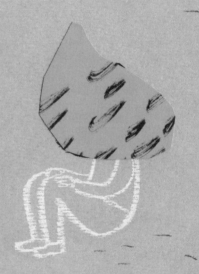

Adapted
into English
by Isol and
Elisa Amado

ENCHANTED LION BOOKS
NEW YORK

THAT'S NOT
AN
ANSWER

aAaA

DOWNPOUR

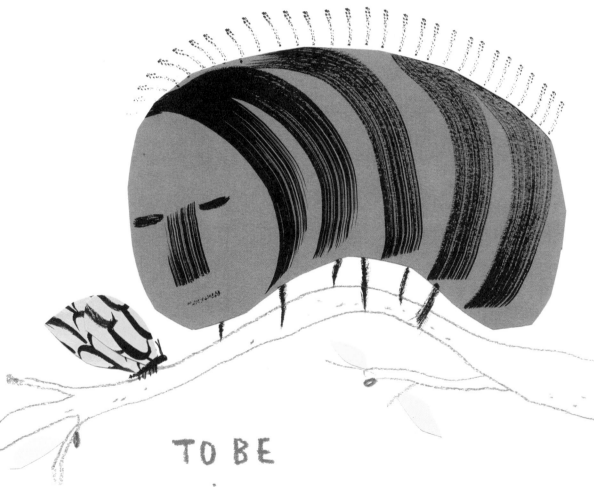

FINE, DON'T SPEAK TO ME

g G g G g

GENTLE
SOUL

HERE
I AM

i I i I

INSOMNIAC

I WAS
JUST
LOOKING
FOR YOU

J J

j j

k K k K

THE KIWI AGAIN!

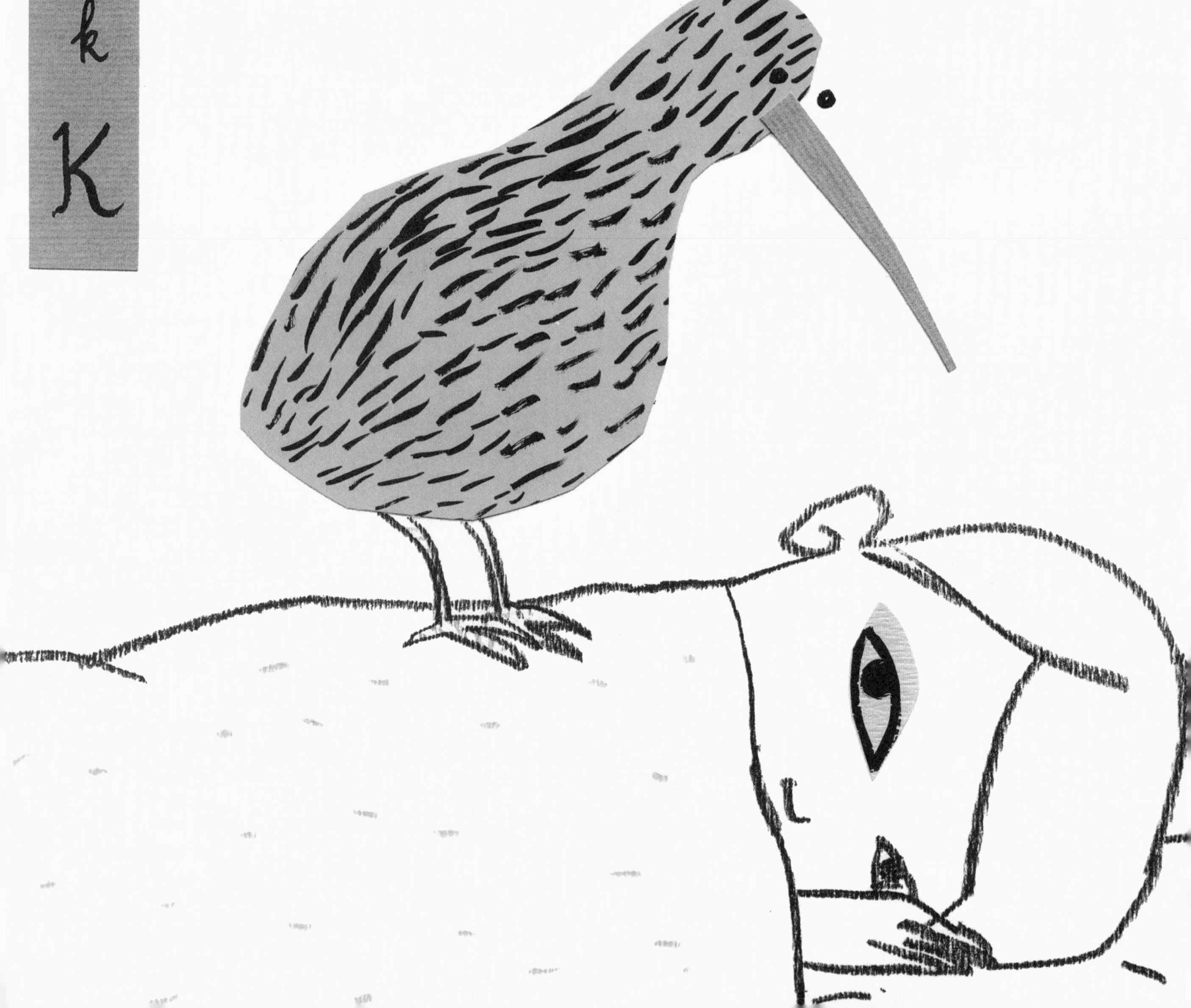

GOOD
MORNING!

m
M
m
m

PROUD

P
P
P
P

q
Q
q
Q

A QUESTION

NEVER MEANT
TO BE RUDE

r
R
r
R

ONE MORE
STEP

GIVE IT
TIME

Ŭ
ŭ

UNEASY

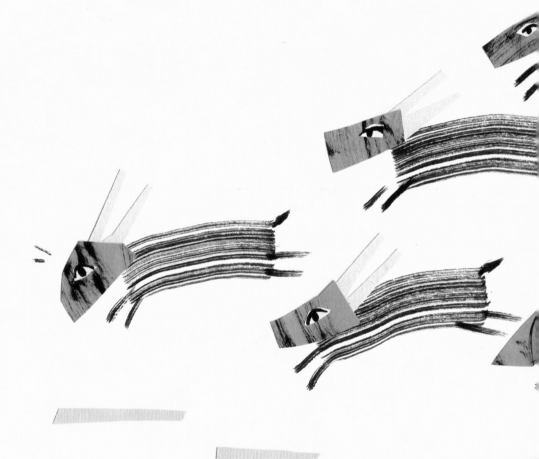

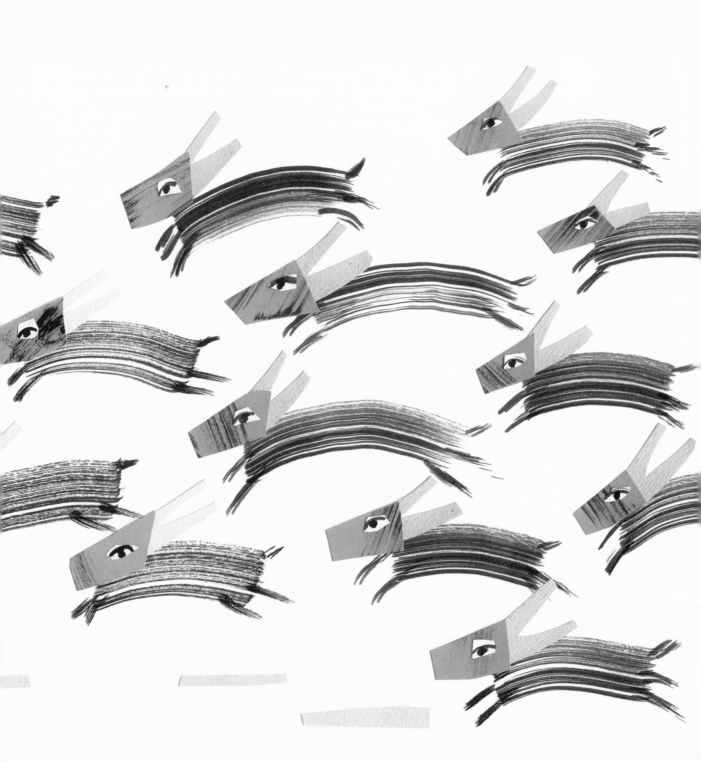

VACATION,
AT LAST!

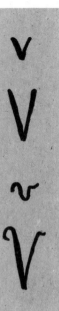

Wow!

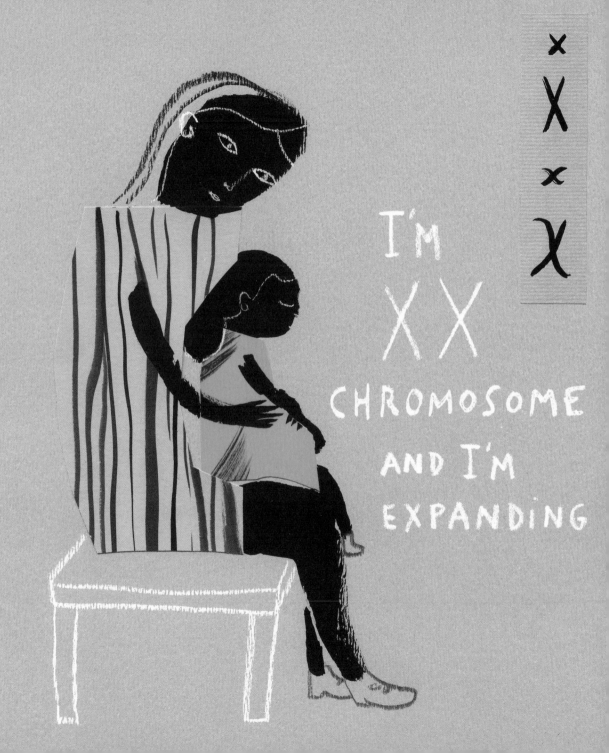

Y Y y y

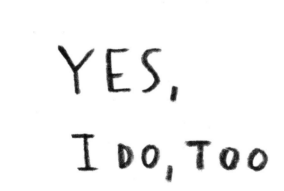

YES,
I DO, TOO

enchantedlionbooks.com

Copyright © 2016 by ISOL for the text & illustrations

First edition published by Enchanted Lion Books,
351 Van Brunt Street, Brooklyn, NY 11231

All rights reserved under International and Pan-American Copyright Conventions
A CIP record is on file with the Library of Congress

ISBN 978-1-59270-195-7

Book design by ISOL

First Edition 2016

This whimsical alphabet is like a game.
For beyond the letters and their sounds, there are
drawings that lead you back to each letter. It was fun
to draw them without thinking about anything other than
their shape and where to put my hand and brush.

This book came into being when I began to play like this:
I started by writing the letters the way I did in school:
first printing them, then in cursive; upper case, lower case.
After, I created images to put beside them. Finally I found the words
to connect them. Words are a wonderful kind of glue.

These images were first created using Spanish letters as Spanish is
my mother tongue. Translating them into English involved a kind
of reinvention. It was fun getting these scenes and characters
to enter into a new conversation in English, where they
found new ways to live together. In this I had a lot of help
from Claudia Zoe Bedrick and Elisa Amado.

When I look at these pages now I see that the letters
have made friends with their images, as though they've
known each other forever. Maybe they really were just
waiting for me to draw them to begin to chat among
themselves and find their reflections in each other.

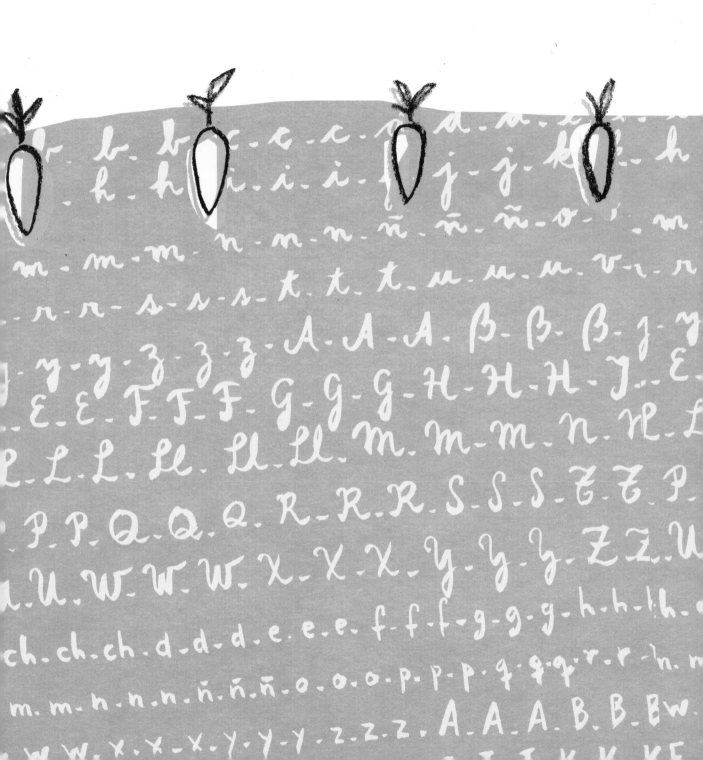

r - r - r - s - N - N

q - q

x - x - y - y - y - z - z - z - A - A

x - x - E - E - E - F - F - F - G - g - g - H - H - H

D - D - D - E - m - m - m - n

K - K - K - L - L - L - L - Ll - Ll - Ll - m

O - O - O - P - P - P - Q - Q - Q - R - R - R - S - S - S - Z

U - U - W - W - W - W - X - X - X - y - y - z

Isol (Argentina, 1972) is one of the most famous authors
and illustrators of children's books in the world.
She has won the Astrid Lindgren Memorial Award,
has twice been selected as a finalist for the Hans Christian Andersen Award
and has won a Golden Apple at the Biennial of Illustration, Bratislava.
With 21 titles published in various languages, her specialty
is narration through the dialogue between image and word.
Isol lives with her family in Buenos Aires.

photo: Stefan Tell